. . . . . WHAT'S AT ISSUE?

CITIZENSHIP & YOU

Katrina Dunbar

Heinemann LIBRARY

www.heinemann.co.uk
Visit our website to find out more information about **Heinemann Library** books.

To order:
☎ Phone 44 (0) 1865 888066
▤ Send a fax to 44 (0) 1865 314091
▢ Visit the Heinemann Bookshop at www.heinemann.co.uk to browse our catalogue and order online.

First published in Great Britain by Heinemann Library, Halley Court, Jordan Hill, Oxford OX2 8EJ, a division of Reed Educational and Professional Publishing Ltd. Heinemann is a registered trademark of Reed Educational & Professional Publishing Limited.

OXFORD MELBOURNE AUCKLAND JOHANNESBURG BLANTYRE
GABORONE IBADAN PORTSMOUTH NH (USA) CHICAGO

Designed by Tinstar Design (www.tinstar.co.uk)
Illustrations by Virginia Gray
Originated by Ambassador Litho Ltd
Printed in Hong Kong/China

04 03 02 01
10 9 8 7 6 5 4 3 2

ISBN 0 431 03545 8

British Library Cataloguing in Publication Data
Dunbar, Katrina
    Citizenship and You. – (What's at issue?)
    1.Citizenship – Juvenile literature
    I.Title
    323.6

Acknowledgements
The author would like to thank Gretchen Marks.
The publishers would like to thank the following for permission to reproduce photographs:
Collections: Nigel French p14; Corbis: pp9, 17, 26, 32, 39; Heinemann: p6; Hulton Getty Images: p18; Oxford Scientific Film: p38; Press Association: p7; Rex Features: pp5, 11, 15, 22, 37; Tony Kyriacou: p36; Sally Greenhill: p30; Sipa Press/Rex Features: p10; Tony Stone Images: pp19, 20, 40, 43
Cover photographs by Still Pictures: Hartmut Schwarzbach

Our thanks to Julie Turner (School Counsellor, Banbury School, Oxfordshire), and to Danièle Spens, JP, for their comments in the preparation of this book.

Every effort has been made to contact copyright holders of any material reproduced in this book. Any omissions will be rectified in subsequent printings if notice is given to the Publisher.

Any words appearing in the text in bold, **like this**, are explained in the Glossary.

Contents

Introduction

The people who are living under a government are known as its citizens. The term 'citizen' comes from ancient Greece, where each city had its own government, with different **laws**. A citizen is a specific kind of person – someone who lives by the system of their government. This book looks at how most citizens in the Western world live together by following laws and taking responsibility for their actions towards each other and their environment.

DEFINITIONS

Citizen: someone who lives in a city or **State**.
Citizenship: the state of being or of having the rights and duties of a citizen.

It looks at how laws are made and what rights we have as citizens. It aims to get you thinking about what citizenship means to you and gives you lots of ideas about how you can actively contribute to improving life for yourself, those who live around you, and people in the wider world.

What is society?

Taking citizenship seriously means knowing what your rights and duties are to yourself, to your fellow countrymen and women, and more generally to other human beings. It means playing a full part in society.

Society is made up of everyone, from all the different neighbourhoods and groups, who are living by the same general rules shaped by the government.

WHAT DOES SOCIETY MEAN TO YOU?

- Grown-ups and rules which I have to follow
- The people I know – my family and friends
- Everyone who lives in my neighbourhood or area.

What is a healthy society?

A healthy society is one in which everybody lives by agreed rules and **laws**, and contributes to helping people live and work together well. The Lord Chancellor, the head of the House of Lords, says: 'A healthy society is made up of people who care about the future – people who reject the "don't care culture", who are not always asking "what's in it for me?"'

Community spirit

When people live and work well together, we call it **community** spirit. Think how an event, such as a weekend festival, a pop concert, a school play, or a sponsored walk for charity, or an ongoing activity such as supporting a football team, gives you a glowing feeling of 'belonging'. People from minority religions and ethnic groups, or who feel they are part of a '**sub-culture**', such as homeless people, may have a strong community spirit with people from the same background. Wouldn't it be amazing if we could all feel like that about belonging to society as a whole?

If society went wrong…

If society completely broke down, and there was no community spirit, no laws and nobody whose job it was to keep the peace, there would be chaos. Imagine what it might be like to try to get through a day like that. Think, for example, how dangerous it feels to be in traffic when one set of traffic lights has broken, and then imagine if there were no rules about keeping within speed limits, stopping for other traffic at road junctions or roundabouts, or stopping at pedestrian crossings for people to cross the road. How many more car accidents would there be?

Give and take in a healthy society

An organization called the Industrial Society ran a big survey in 1997 called the *2020 Vision Programme*. It gathered the views of 12–25 year-olds, who would be the decision-makers by the year 2020. It found that young people named stability and opportunity as the keys to a healthy society. Opportunity means a chance of having rewarding and enjoyable work, and is important because work gives people a sense of worth and achievement, and this contributes to society. Stability means a neighbourhood free from crime, with everybody respecting everyone else's way of life. How healthy do you think our society is?

Notting Hill Carnival is an annual weekend festival, started by the West Indian community living in that part of London. Young and older people from many different backgrounds dance and celebrate community spirit.

What is a good citizen?

People may think of themselves as good citizens because they never break the **law**, never disturb their neighbours, and keep themselves to themselves. But is this enough? Citizenship means much more than this. There is a lot of debate, especially in the **media** and the government, about needing to encourage people to play a more 'active' part in society. What does this mean?

> If I see a little kid throw their rubbish on the floor, I say 'hey' and 'put it in the bin'.

Young adult giving one example of how he plays an 'active' part in society.

SYREETA'S STORY

Syreeta's story is a good example. As she was leaving home for school, she heard her next door neighbour's burglar alarm go off. She had never met them, but knocked on their door anyway. No reply. Even though she was in a wheelchair and could not move quickly, she came home, telephoned the police and reported it. That was an act of good citizenship because Syreeta showed that she cared about her **community** and the people who live in it beyond her immediate social circle, and she acted in a responsible way to improve a situation.

Taking action

Being a good citizen means not doing things which hurt other people or the environment, such as dropping litter or spray-painting graffiti that somebody else will have to clean off. But it also means doing your bit 'to make the world a better place'. Young people are especially good at putting creative energy into improving their environment – you do not have to be an adult to be a good citizen. Can you remember when you last did something which showed you were a good citizen?

Active citizenship is about enjoying your rights and accepting that these bring responsibilities. In 1998, the UK Prime Minister, Tony Blair, said: 'This is not the something for nothing society.' For example, as we see later in this book, the right to vote for the government means that you have to think carefully about who you believe is best for the job. In order that every citizen can have the right to a fair trial if they are accused of committing a crime, as an adult you may be called to serve on a jury (which decides whether somebody is guilty or not).

FACT

● *40% of young people aged 16–24 showed they cared about people and communities beyond their own social circle. They had recently made a donation to charity.*

> The State of the Young Nation *survey by the British Youth Council in July 1998*

Representatives of the Children's Parliament show what it means to be active citizens by taking their proposals for saving the planet to the top people in government.

THE CHILDREN'S PARLIAMENT ON THE ENVIRONMENT

In May 1999, a group of 60 10- and 11-year-old 'citizens' from schools all over England were given the opportunity to debate their ideas on the future of the environment, to question the Deputy Prime Minister, John Prescott, and the Speaker of the House of Commons, Betty Boothroyd, and to present ten points for action to the Prime Minister at Downing Street. The children were chosen through schools taking part in debating and essay writing competitions. In exchange for the children taking seriously their role as citizens who care about the planet, John Prescott promised: 'The government will seriously consider the recommendations… and their place in new laws which will ensure the future health of the Earth.'

Rules – are they there to be broken?

The **media** often describes a new band or fashion as 'breaking all the rules'. This means they think it is exciting, refreshing and rebellious. The word 'rules' suggests boring and restricting regulations, but a healthy society needs some rules and **laws** so that citizens can live harmoniously together. Citizens over the age of 18 are all responsible for voting in the government, whose job it is to create the laws.

Why have any rules at all?

Are rules at home and school just adults' way of bossing children about and stopping them from being individuals? Or can rules be helpful? Do you agree with this young person's opinion, which comes from the National Children's Bureau's *Young Opinions, Great Ideas* survey: 'I think that the children should have a say in the rules and it shouldn't just be the parents' point of view of what you should and shouldn't do. I think that children should put down some rules for them as well'.

Some of your school's rules may seem petty, but there may be a reason for them that you haven't thought of. For example, some schools have a rule which bans personal stereos and mobile phones. One of the main reasons for this is that they want pupils to concentrate on lessons so that they achieve good results and have the best opportunities when they leave school.

Do you think that school uniform is a good idea? If everyone has to wear the same school uniform, it is not so obvious that some people have more money and it encourages everybody to feel equal. Sensible rules can make people feel safer and happier, because they know what is expected of them, and it is clear when others are being out of order.

Keeping you safe

Both in school and outside, rules and laws are intended to protect you from yourself and others. Sometimes they are really a warning, for example shops are not allowed to sell cigarettes to anyone under the age of sixteen because they are so bad for your health. There are always big lists of rules at swimming pools, which aim to prevent accidents. Speed restrictions on roads and rules about not driving if you have drunk alcohol are there to save lives and avoid accidents.

CASE STUDY: RULES

At Phoenix School in West London, pupils were so disruptive that the school nearly had to be closed. A new head teacher was appointed over the Easter holidays, who created rules, including a school uniform that pupils had to wear, and a clear discipline system. A year later, pupils were getting much higher exam results and the school was a safe **community**, where pupils said they felt more relaxed and happy.

If everybody had enough money, and everything they needed to have a good quality of life, do you think we would still need laws? The only thing that seems to stop some people from breaking the rules and committing crimes is fear of going to prison. Can you think of a situation where you think more rules or laws are needed?

This overturned car is a shocking warning of what can happen if somebody breaks the law about not driving after drinking alcohol – rules and laws can save lives.

Groups – who's to blame for group actions?

How much do you think you are influenced by your friends? Do you think there is a lot of **peer** pressure? Peer pressure means pressure to join in with what your group of friends is doing, even if on your own, you might choose to do something else.

All for one, and one for all

In a group or gang, people take up roles and may do things that they would not dare to do if they were on their own. This can be positive – you often hear footballers say that they performed better than they had ever imagined because the team members were spurring each other on, for example. Often people will make more effort, or even take a risk because they want to impress their group and not let them down.

Peer pressure can lead to people taking risks which they feel are wrong and even dangerous. There have been several cases in the **media** of teenagers taking drugs amongst friends at a party, and being dead by the morning. Their personal history usually reveals that they would never have dreamt of taking such a risk if it had not been for peer pressure. Sometimes they are later shown to have had a medical condition that they have chosen to ignore in order to be 'one of the gang'! Would you want to risk your life just to impress your mates?

It stops being healthy to be part of a group or gang when the group or dominant individuals in it bring out the worst behaviour and attitudes in each other rather than the best. A big risk of groups is that power may go to the heads of the leaders, and the rest of the group follow, like sheep, without questioning their ideas. Some people think of a religious **cult** such as the **Moonies** as being like this, because followers only mix with other Moonies, cut themselves off from their family, follow strict rules and give up expressing themselves as individuals.

Members of a religious cult called the Moonies take part in a wedding ceremony in the USA. Thousands of couples, who may not have met before, do this to show their devotion to Reverend Moon.

The Hell's Angels have an instantly recognizable 'look' and a 'tough' image. Local 'chapters' of bikers set up in its name throughout the Western world see themselves as a **sub-culture** in society.

Individual responsibility

Should soldiers be held personally responsible for acts they commit as part of an army? During the Second World War, which ended in 1945, German army officers were horrifyingly cruel towards Jewish prisoners. Some of those officers are still being tried now, nearly half a century later, in a special court for war crimes. When a group crime of any kind has been committed, the courts look at each individual's role in it and deal out punishment accordingly. Do you think this is right?

Standing up for others in a group situation

What do you do if you hear one of your class mates shouting a **racist** comment? Do you think that by keeping quiet you are making yourself as bad as they are?

FACT

● *50% of 11–16 year-olds responding to a survey believed that friends' attitudes can help to prevent young people from becoming involved in crime.*

2020 Vision survey by the Industrial Society, 1997

These words from Pastor Martin Niemaller, a German prisoner in the Second World War, are often used by the **pressure group** Amnesty International to show what an important part of citizenship it is to challenge wrongdoing:

In Germany they first came for the Communists; I did not speak because I was not a Communist. Then they came for the Jews; I did not speak because I was not a Jew. Afterward, they came for the Catholics; I did not say anything because I was a Protestant. Eventually they came for me, and there was no one left to speak.

Duty calls – grassing versus loyalty

Is a true friend a loyal friend?

We all feel that we should stand by our friends, no matter what, but sometimes that is not possible or even the right thing to do. In criminal circles a 'grass' is the lowest form of life, and criminals who are known to have given the police information that has led to others being arrested often have to be locked up separately from other prisoners for their own safety.

Imagine a situation at school where you know that a friend of yours has stolen somebody else's Nike shoes out of their locker. It is reported and someone in the class, who has a reputation for being a thief, is accused by the teacher. What do you do?

a) Think 'well, so and so often does steal things, so they are just getting what they deserve' and keep quiet.

b) Sneakily tell someone else, so that the truth can come out without your friend knowing you grassed on them.

When is it right to speak up?

Whatever our different religious and cultural beliefs, most of us have a strong sense of right and wrong from an early age. Part of being an active citizen is standing up for what you believe to be right, even if you are risking losing a friend or the approval of most of your **peers**.

Bullying

Bullying can easily divide people's loyalties. You may be worried that if you speak up when you see someone bullying someone else, you will be the next victim.

If a friend is being bullied at school or home, they may be too frightened or ashamed to report it to an adult. They may ask you to promise not to tell anyone. Is it OK to 'grass' because a friend is suffering in silence?

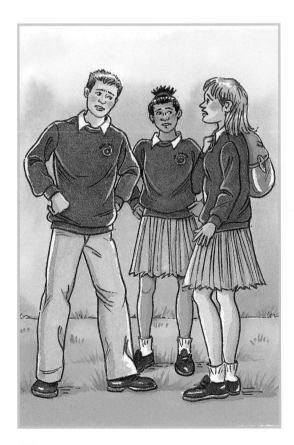

C) Tell your friend that if they don't own up to stealing the shoes, you will have to report them. You may lose the friendship, but this has made you wonder whether you want them as a friend anyway.

WHAT TO DO IF A FRIEND IS BEING BULLIED

● Be there for them to talk about it – your friendship is especially important at times like this.

● Encourage them to tell a teacher, a parent or **carer**, a friendly adult, or ring Childline to talk about it. (see 'Contacts and helplines' on pages 46–7). Maybe your school has an anti-bullying campaign like Acland Burghley in London (see page 40).

● If it is a school situation, you could confront the bullies and threaten that you will report them. Think carefully, though, whether this is putting your own safety at risk.

● If your friend is too frightened to speak up, talk to a responsible adult yourself.

FACTS

● *Childline gets 20,000 calls a year from schoolchildren who are being bullied.*
● *10% (1 in 10) pupils in secondary school are bullied.*
● *Kate Winslet, Anthea Turner, Martin Clunes and Prince Naseem Hamed were all bullied at school.*

Police – keeping society peaceful

We need the police to keep the peace in society. They are the people we all rely on to do their best to ensure that people do not break the **law**, and to arrest anybody that they discover doing so. Their job is very varied. One day they might be in the background at a gathering where a crowd could get out of hand, such as at a public demonstration. The next they might be responding to a 999 emergency call and chasing burglars over garden fences to arrest them.

People have very different views of the police – some people feel safe when they see officers walking around their neighbourhood, especially older people. Others feel as if they are being spied on immediately they see the uniform. How do you feel?

Police powers and duties

The police are allowed to stop people, and search them, if they think they are carrying illegal drugs, stolen goods, or a weapon of any kind.

There are strict **guidelines**, drawn up by the government, which the police have to follow when they are investigating crime. These are known as the Codes of Practice.

FACTS

- *Most of the information the police receive when investigating crime comes from the public.*
- *The police can take fingerprints of anyone over the age of ten whom they believe to be involved in a crime.*
- *If a police officer stops you in the street, you have the right to know their name, number and the police station where they work.*
- *People are less likely to re-offend if they get a caution from the police rather than going to court.*

Police are an important presence ensuring that people feel safe at crowded public events, such as the annual Trooping the Colour in London.

What to do if the police stop you

You must keep calm and be polite – staying calm will help you to keep thinking straight. Do not do anything to deliberately mislead the police or waste their time, since this is an imprisonable offence.

Questioning

If the police approach you and want to take you to the station for questioning, remember that anyone under 17 should not be interviewed without a parent or adult friend or teacher there.

What next?

If the police think you have committed a crime they may charge you, so that you go to court (see pages 16–17). Depending on how serious the crime is and if you have admitted to it, they may give you a formal caution. A caution is a strong warning from a senior police officer,

Sometimes police use 'full riot gear' in order to break up situations where groups of angry people have got out of control, perhaps at a public demonstration.

reminding you that you will go to court if you commit further offences. A final warning scheme is now being tried out for under 18 year-olds, which replaces cautioning and is aimed at giving young people more of a chance to avoid court.

RULES FOR THE POLICE

The Codes of Practice are broken if a police officer:

- neglects their duty without a good reason
- misuses their authority, perhaps through violence
- makes a false statement
- is rude to a member of the public
- behaves in a **racist** way.

The law – is it a fair system?

We have looked at why rules and **laws** are necessary. In Britain, any citizen who is accused of breaking the law has the right to a fair trial in court. The law says you are 'presumed innocent until proven guilty'.

Types of court and how they work

There are three main types of court in Britain.

Magistrates' Court

Many magistrates are not lawyers, but members of the public who have been chosen because they are good citizens. They are also called justices of the peace, and there are normally three of them in court. They reach a decision, known as a verdict, on less serious cases, for example where somebody has been caught driving a car which is deemed to be unfit for the road, but where nobody has been hurt, or where somebody has been caught for not paying a bus fare and refused to pay the on-the-spot fine. Magistrates decide whether a case is serious enough to go to the Crown Court, though at present the defendant (person accused) can insist on going to the Crown Court.

Crown Court

A judge oversees the trial, makes sure that the case is fairly presented and decides on the level of punishment if someone is found guilty once all the **evidence** is heard. The main difference in a Crown Court, as opposed to a Magistrates' Court, is that a jury (made up of 12 local citizens) decides whether someone is guilty or not. Hearing the case involves listening to a lawyer prosecuting (setting out why somebody is guilty), and another defending (arguing for their innocence). The defendant is questioned by both lawyers. The police and other people may also be questioned as witnesses. Trials can take a few days or several months.

Youth, or Juvenile, Court

This is a special court for people under the age of 18, although anybody accused of a crime as serious as murder, for example, will go to trial in a Crown Court. There are three magistrates in a Youth Court, who are trained to deal with young people. If someone is under 16, their parents or a **carer** must be at the court with them.

Adults may go and listen to cases at Magistrates' and Crown Courts, but Youth Courts are closed to the public. There are strict laws about how the **media** reports cases before and during a trial. In the case of Stephen Lawrence, a black teenager who was murdered in London in April 1993, the young men suspected of his murder may not be brought back to court despite new evidence, for example, because it might be an unfair trial. This is due to media attention, which could **prejudice** the jury.

The Old Bailey is England's oldest Crown Court. Wigs are still worn by the judge and barristers, so the scene today would not be very different from this old illustration.

THE JURY

Most citizens over the age of 18 will be called to be on a jury at least once in their lifetime. It is one of the only compulsory duties of a citizen in Britain. Juries were introduced in the fifteenth century to make sure that trials were fair. However, the government wants to change the law so that defendants can no longer choose between a trial by jury and a magistrates court. It says that the magistrates should decide, rather than the defendant, and that time and money could be saved. The House of Lords rejected the idea because it reduces citizens' rights. What do you think?

THE AGE OF LEGAL RESPONSIBILITY

The law says that children under 10 years-old are too young to be responsible if they break the law, although they may be put into a special care centre by a youth court in extreme cases, such as murder. A new Act of Parliament, the Crime and Disorder Act of 1998, recently changed the law so that young people between the ages of 10 and 13 are now held responsible for their actions, and boys under 14 can be tried for crimes of a sexual nature. At what age do you think youngsters are ready to take responsibility for their own actions?

Children's rights

In the nineteenth century, many people supported Queen Victoria's view that 'children should be seen and not heard'. In numerous novels from this period such as *Jane Eyre* by Charlotte Bronte and *Oliver Twist* by Charles Dickens, the main character was cruelly treated as a child. Children who were not protected by their parents or by wealth were **exploited** as cheap labour, famously being sent up chimneys or down mines into life-threatening conditions. Towards the end of the nineteenth century, **laws** were gradually introduced to protect children, and the twentieth century has seen a growing respect for children as citizens with certain rights.

Your right to be an individual

Article 12 of the UN Convention on the Rights of the Child states that where at all possible the child's opinion should be heard and taken into account. Some

people say there should be a law giving children the right to be consulted about everything important that happens in their family. Do you think that would work in this country?

You have the right to a name, nationality and birthday under Article 7. You have the right to live with your parents unless it is not in your best interests under Article 9 – you have the right to keep in contact with both your parents even if you cannot live with them. You also have the right to all information about you, such as school files and adoption papers under Articles 17 and 21. Organizations like Save the Children and the National Children's Bureau can tell you more about this (see 'Contacts and helplines' on pages 46–7).

Laws have gradually been created to protect children from being used as cheap labour, like this young factory worker in 1910.

Your right to protection

Articles 19 and 20 make it the State's duty to protect you from abuse and **neglect**, either at home or in **care**. Article 22 gives **refugees** the same protection.

Several articles aim to protect children from exploitation. Article 32 makes the **State** responsible for setting a minimum working age and acceptable conditions of work. You should also be protected from **drug abuse**, **sexual exploitation**, being sold or **abducted**, and from being caught up in war.

The UN Convention is not enforceable in the courts, but is a set of good standards which every country interprets and supports in their own way with national laws. In the UK, the 1989 Children Act gives clear guidance on State protection of children, especially from abuse, and states that the **local council** must house children who are homeless, for example. The Children Act does not protect anyone over the age of 16.

Abuse

As well as clear laws, there are several organizations which exist to help children who are being hurt, or neglected. They recognize that abusers are often the child's own family, who should be the child's first line of protection in society. Abuse means different things to different people, but if you are worried that you are being badly treated you could contact Childline, the National Society for the Protection of Cruelty to Children NSPCC (see 'Contacts and helplines' on pages 46–7), the police, the social services department of your local council, or talk to any responsible adult as a first step.

Children's rights to be listened to and respected are part of a detailed list of 40 rights and protections in the United Nations (UN) Convention on the Rights of the Child.

FACTS

● *In the mid-nineteenth century, 50% of all children died before the age of 10 from illnesses which typically occur when children live or work in bad conditions.*

● *There are up to 400 million child labourers throughout the world today. These children are denied education, play, rest and social life. The vast majority live in the developing world.*

from Invisible Children, *survey by Save the Children, 1997*

● *121 children under the age of 16 were killed in the war in Northern Ireland between 1969 and 1994.*

A Guide to Rights, *Save the Children, 1994*

● *95% of children calling Childline about sexual or physical abuse know the abuser. In other words the abuser is a family member or friend, or a familiar acquaintance.*

Do we really have equal rights?

Laws exist which give all citizens equal rights. This means the same rights to employment and a home, for example. We are all born with different skills and personalities – so is it really possible to treat everybody equally?

The diversity of people who make up society is one of its greatest assets, yet one of our biggest challenges for the next century is to achieve genuine equality for all citizens.

George Orwell's famous book *Animal Farm* follows the overthrow of a farmer by his animals. In their new life, the pigs slowly claim more and more power until they even start wearing the farmer's clothes. Their view is that: 'All animals are equal, but some are more equal than others.' This is Orwell's tongue-in-cheek way of saying that some humans believe they are superior to others.

Society does not treat everybody equally

Most people say they believe that society should value the variety of backgrounds, and the physical and personality differences of the groups and individuals that enrich it. However, all of us see daily examples in the **media** and our own lives of certain groups being treated as less important than others. It may be because of their colour, sex, **sexuality**, religion, language, some form of disability or physical features, or because they are a child or an old person.

Prejudice

Racism is a good example of **prejudice**. Racism is the act of treating somebody from a different race differently because of prejudice, and is illegal behaviour. People from all races commit racism, and there is a seemingly endless list of grudges, for example Scots against English and vice versa, or some white Australians against the Aborigines.

There has been a history of prejudice against women in the workplace. The Sex **Discrimination** Act makes it illegal for **employers** to treat men and women differently, but women still find that they hit a 'glass ceiling' which stops them climbing beyond a certain level of seniority within some companies.

Fear and ignorance

Many people have prejudices because they are frightened of what they do not know. People often take on the **racist** views of their parents and certain **tabloid** newspapers without questioning them. Targeting a group with hatred is the way some people avoid feeling insecure about themselves and their own background.

Gay and lesbian people are often targeted by people who are unsure of their own **sexuality**.

Opportunities rather than automatic rights

While many people claim they want everybody to be treated equally, most people mean that they want everyone to have the same chances, or equal opportunities. If two people apply for a job, for example, neither of them has an automatic right to the job, only to be considered equally for their suitability. The one with the most relevant skills and experience is the one who is most likely to get the job.

FACTS

- *Young people from **ethnic minorities** are almost twice as likely to be unemployed as their white peers.*
- *60% of British people would marry someone from another race, or be happy for their children to do so.*

Survey by the helpline charity Childline

CASE STUDY: TACKLING RACIST VIOLENCE

South Camden Community School is in one of the most deprived inner-city areas of London, and has a reputation for racist violence. It has tackled the problem by establishing a project which is led by the young people themselves. The group includes Bengalis, Nigerians, Eritreans, Somalians and Turkish people. They work out solutions to the immediate problems in school, and work with youth and community leaders to educate their **peers** about their experience of racism.

Protecting human rights

'Human rights' is a broad term meaning the right to be treated with respect as a fellow human being in all circumstances.

Convention on Human Rights

Hitler and the Nazis' persecution and killing of millions of Jewish people during the Second World War led to the drawing up of the Convention on Human Rights in 1953. It is a list of very basic rights and freedoms, a right to a fair trial, freedom of thought, religion, **sexuality**, and the freedom to express your opinions in public. They are the kinds of rights that have been **abused** by all countries,

These Kosovan refugees are like thousands of people all over the world who are forced to flee their homes in fear of their lives, because of people in power who ignore human rights.

including the UK, in past centuries. **Pressure groups** like Amnesty International try to persuade governments all over the world to adopt and enforce human rights. It is easy for most people in the UK to take them for granted these days, but some of the **refugees** living in the UK today have fled their own country with their lives in danger because of the political opinions they expressed, for example.

Britain is in the process of including the Convention on Human Rights into the Human Rights Act, which becomes law during 2000.

A special court to protect human rights

The European Court of Human Rights in Strasbourg (France) hears cases where people feel their rights have been ignored under the Convention. The process is complicated and it takes a long time for cases to come to court. The claimant (the person making the claim or complaint) must show that they have already used every possible route in their own country before bringing their complaint to the European Court. If the court agrees that the Convention has been broken, governments must comply with the decision and will probably have to pay a sum of money to compensate the claimant, known as 'damages', as well as the costs of bringing the case to court.

Decisions made by the European Court

There have been some major historic decisions made by the European Court that have had a lasting effect in Britain. The European Court:
- condemned corporal punishment in schools, which led to Britain largely abolishing it in 1987
- criticized the treatment of suspected **terrorists** in Northern Ireland
- allowed prisoners the right to have private correspondence with their lawyers
- declared British **immigration** rules were unlawful because they did not treat men and women equally.

CASE STUDY: HUMAN RIGHTS

Imagine sitting around the television with your family when soldiers burst through the front door and grab you... The Lord's Resistance Army, in northern Uganda, has taken between 5000 and 8000 children away from their families by force since 1995. It has made them join the army, even though many do not even understand why they are fighting. Often they are beaten or tortured by other soldiers as part of their training. Uganda is not the only country which abuses human rights by using children in this way.

GROUP ACTION

Amnesty International has 250 school groups around the country, who are part of their Urgent Action Scheme. Young campaigners write letters to governments worldwide to ask them to release people who are in prison because of their political beliefs.

FACTS

- *1 in every 255 people on the planet is a refugee, and the majority are women and children.*
- *Up to 1998 the European Court had received more appeals against Britain than any other country.*
- *More appeals are won against Britain than any other country.*

So who makes the laws?

Just as the head teacher and governors set some basic rules to ensure that your school runs smoothly and everybody knows how they are expected to behave, Parliament sets the **laws** and **policies** needed to ensure that more than 50 million people can live together in the UK. It is Parliament that decides everything from what subjects children should learn at school, to the maximum speed limit for driving on motorways, to what **currency** is used.

Parliament

Parliament is made up of the House of Commons and the House of Lords (see pages 28–9) and has been developing into its current form since King John signed an agreement called the Magna Carta at Runnymede, Surrey, in 1216. This limited the power and responsibility of the **monarchy** for the first time. The most influential people were called upon regularly for advice, with such gatherings known as 'parlements', from the French verb 'parler', 'to speak'.

Making laws

Between 50 and 60 major new laws are passed by Parliament every year. The detailed process described below means that it can take years for an idea that was in an **election manifesto** to become an Act of Parliament.

Drafting a bill

Government **ministers** and **civil servants** consult experts and advisory groups as they are drafting a bill. They may test what the public think through **opinion polls** and by publicizing their ideas in the **media**. Sometimes a Green Paper is published to formally ask people what they think. This is the stage that **lobbying** from **pressure groups** can be most effective, because ideas are not yet firmly established. Before the 1996 Housing Act became law, for example, the homelessness charity Shelter ran a campaign which led to 10,000 responses to the Green Paper – a record number. The final Act did give homeless people more protection than the Green Paper had proposed.

The next stage is to publish a White Paper. This is the bill that goes through a set parliamentary process (see page 25).

Private Member's Bills

As well as public bills, individual Members of Parliament (MPs) can introduce Private Member's Bills. Mike Foster MP's bill to ban fox hunting is an example of this. Such bills highlight issues very well, even if they do not become law, because they are debated by Parliament and the media.

> ## *FACTS*
>
> ● *Young people aged 10–17 told a survey they thought they should have a say in new laws and government decisions that affect them.*
>
> > *Young Opinions, Great Ideas survey by the National Children's Bureau, 1998*
>
> ● *See pages 42–3 for ideas about how you can have a say!*

FROM BILL TO ACT

FIRST READING

formal announcement of the bill.

SECOND READING

a full debate in the House of Commons.

STANDING COMMITTEE

this consists of 16–20 MPs, who look carefully at each clause (section or paragraph) of the bill and may make alterations.

THIRD READING

this is the point when the government may respond to public pressure or opposition parties by altering the bill. The House of Commons then votes on whether to approve it.

HOUSE OF LORDS

the bill goes through the same process as in the House of Commons. Any alterations requested means the bill gets returned to the Commons.

ROYAL ASSENT

the Queen puts her signature to the bill to turn it into an Act of Parliament.

Who chooses the government?

One of the most important responsibilities of a citizen is to help choose the government.

Elections

All citizens over the age of 18 have the right to vote by secret **ballot** for one **candidate** to represent their local area in the national government. The government is formed by the political party whose candidates get the most votes in a general election. These are held once every five years – you may have seen a **polling station** set up in your school.

There is usually a choice of three people to vote for, one from each of the three main political parties. The candidates who win the most votes become Members of Parliament (known as MPs) and work in the House of Commons (see pages 28–9). Do you know who your local MP is and which political party they represent?

People talk to representatives of political parties outside their local polling station as they wait to vote – every citizen over the age of 18 has the right to take part in electing the government.

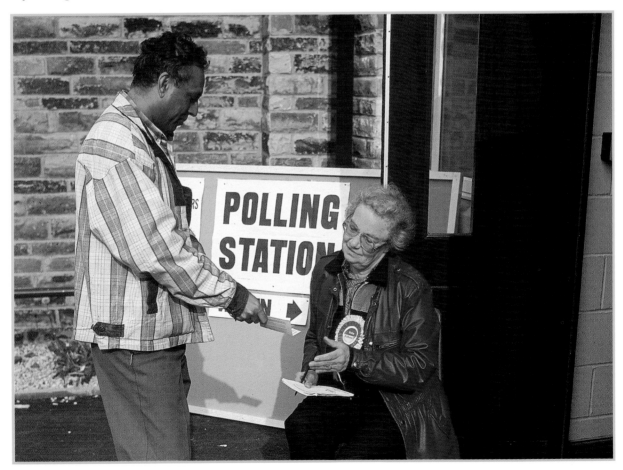

Political parties

Political parties are organized groups of people who share the same general views about how the country should be run. There are three main parties in Britain – the Conservative Party, the Labour Party, and the Liberal Democrat Party. Other parties in the UK include the Green Party and the Independent Party. Political parties select candidates for elections, train them in political processes and give them advice. They also raise money to pay for public meetings and promote their **policies**. Political parties have regular Party Political Broadcasts on television and radio, especially in the months before a general election.

You can join a political party when you are 18. Does anybody in your family belong to a political party? Which party does your family vote for in elections? Do they all vote for the same party?

FACTS

- *24% of British adults voted in the European elections in 1999, compared with 75% in the general election.*
- *28% of 11–16 year-olds told a 1999 Mori/Guardian* **opinion poll** *that they want more political education. Every school will have Citizenship taught as part of the national curriculum by 2002, which will include teaching about* **politics***.*

SCHOOL COUNCILS CAN WORK LIKE GOVERNMENT

School councils are increasingly common in secondary schools in the UK. At Ashley Special School in Widnes, Cheshire, the school council has a number of committees, so that most pupils can be involved if they want to be. The council meets once a month together with school governors. Pupils vote at a polling station set up in the local community centre. Pupils have been to the House of Commons, the House of Lords and to Brussels to talk to MPs and MEPs (Members of the European Parliament).

But how well do school councils work? A survey done by the University of London's Institute of Education, in November 1999, questioned nearly 2300 pupils aged between 7 and 17, and found that most young people wanted to contribute more to their school community, and be recognized as competent and responsible. Half the pupils said that they did have a school council, but only one in five thought that it was effective. Only one quarter believed that their teachers take their opinions seriously, and 40% felt they should have more rights in school. Only 11% of teachers agreed with this view. One pupil said: 'I think that children need to be treated like adults more, because it is only the age that is different. Everyone has opinions whether they are 10 or 40, it doesn't matter. Everyone still has rights to say what they believe.' Do you agree? Why don't you ask to have a class debate about how you could get your views taken more seriously by your school?

The people in Parliament

House of Commons

There are 659 Members of Parliament (MPs) in the House of Commons. In the 1997 general election, 419 of those voted in were members of the Labour Party, which then formed the government. MPs from **opposition parties** have an important role as new **laws** are being made and to keep the government in check. If you visit the House of Commons

This video still shows the first meeting of Parliament with the new MPs after the general election in 2001.

to watch a debate, or see it on the television, you will notice how lively the atmosphere can be. The Speaker of the House leads a procession into the debating chamber at the start of the day's work and MPs have to address each other by their formal title 'the honourable member'. In contrast, debates can get so noisy that the Speaker has to knock on the floor with her mace, calling: 'Order, order'!

Prime Minister

The Prime Minister is head of the House of Commons, leader of their political party and leader of the government. His or her biggest challenge in the House of Commons is Prime Minister's Question Time – a lively twice weekly session when MPs from the opposition parties and sometimes the Prime Minister's own cross examine him or her on **policy**.

House of Lords

Members of the House of Lords have never been voted for by the public, but the way they become members is undergoing reform. Until autumn 1999, there was a mixture of hereditary Lords (who have inherited the title through their family), life peers (who are made Lords for their lifetime by the Prime Minister), bishops, archbishops and Law Lords (judges). There are around a thousand Lords, but life peers tend to be the most actively involved in the House of Lords. The government is considering **abolishing** the House of Lords altogether, believing that the whole government should be democratically elected. As a first step, it has replaced hereditary Lords with Lords elected by each of the politcal parties. Do you think this is a good idea?

SCOTLAND AND WALES

In 1997, the new UK Labour government held a special vote, called a referendum, amongst the citizens of Scotland and Wales to give them the choice of having their own parliaments. Since 1998 and 1999 respectively, both countries have elected their own MPs and they now have the power to make their own policies and laws about matters which do not need to be UK wide. These include education, housing and the countryside. Some issues, known as reserved matters, are still dealt with by the UK Parliament. These include defence and foreign policy.

EUROPEAN PARLIAMENT

This is based in Brussels (Belgium) and Strasbourg (France) and has 626 members (MEPs) elected from the 15 countries in the **European Union** – in Britain we elect ours in the same way as MPs. The European Parliament, European Commission and Council of Ministers together create European Law, which concentrates on the environment, agriculture, transport and **civil liberties**.

PART-TIME CLEANER OBTAINS JUSTICE

The European Equal Opportunities Commission helped a part-time cleaner who got no pay when she was made **redundant** to win her court case. Judges said that the principle of European Law, that men and women should be treated equally, was broken by not giving part-time workers (who were mainly women) the same rights as full-time workers. As a result UK law changed to give all workers the same protection.

Governing your neighbourhood

We have already seen how national government, based at the Houses of Parliament in Westminster, makes decisions for Britain as a whole. Your village, town or city also has its own local government, which people usually refer to as the council.

The public baths you swim in, your local library and park are all there because of your local council. Local government makes a big difference to your everyday life and you can get involved in the decisions it makes.

What does local government do?

Local government is crucial to making the difference between a healthy and an unhealthy society. An example of this is tackling crime. **Opinion polls** regularly show that the biggest worry amongst people of all ages is wanting to feel safer from crime. National government makes **laws** and **policies** which aim to reduce crime, but it is your **local council** which ensures that dark alleyways are well lit and that there are security cameras in public places and on housing estates. They invest huge amounts of time and money in planning the lay-out of public areas for maximum safety, so that people can feel part of a thriving **community** rather than live in fear.

Your everyday needs

Certain areas of life, such as health, are dealt with by separate government organizations, known as quangos, but local government works in partnership with national government to provide many of the everyday services. This includes making sure you have somewhere to live, that you get an education, that there is transport to get about on, that libraries, leisure facilities and parks are established, that your rubbish gets collected and recycled, your street gets cleaned, and providing what are known as social services – this includes children's homes, and services (such as meals on wheels for older people).

Who is your local government?

Your local government, or council, is run by councillors, who are elected by all citizens aged 18 or over, every four years, using the same voting method as for MPs. Councillors are from a political party, like MPs. Do you know who your local councillors are, or which political party is leading your council?

Councillors make the decisions, but the work of the council is carried out by officers, who are employed by the council. There is also a Mayor, who is a councillor elected by the other councillors for a period of four years. The Mayor's duty is to represent the council and attend openings of new buildings and events such as local fêtes.

How can you get involved?

Local government aims to be truly **democratic** and involve local citizens. All the major decisions about what happens in your neighbourhood are made at committee meetings of councillors. They take place in the Town Hall and anybody can go along. You can find out what is being discussed and ask to send what is called a 'deputation' – this is a group of people affected by a topic under discussion.

CASE STUDY: HAVING YOUR SAY

A council was about to close two youth clubs and open two new ones. After listening to a group of teenagers explaining how important one of the clubs was to them at a committee meeting, the councillors decided to keep the clubs open for at least six more months and to plan the move to new clubs differently. Is there anything that you would like your local council to do differently?

God Save The Queen?

The **monarchy** has not had any real political power in Britain for hundreds of years.

The royal loss of power

The death of Diana, Princess of Wales, in a car crash in Paris in 1997, re-ignited a longstanding argument that the Royal Family is outdated and should be **abolished**. Yet many people love the 'Royals' and millions watch a royal wedding or the Queen's Speech on Christmas Day.

Should we abolish the royal family?

What do you think? How might you change the Royal Family to make them fit in better with today's society?

AUSTRALIAN HEAD OF STATE

The Queen of England, Elizabeth II, is also Queen of Australia. The Australian Governor-General carries out political duties as the Queen's representative. In November 1999 Australia held a nationwide referendum to ask the people whether they wanted to replace the Queen as head of State with a President, elected by Parliament. This would make Australia a republic like the United States of America. Almost 55% of the electorate rejected the idea, despite a nine-year campaign by keen republicans.

SHOULD WE ABOLISH

YES:
- They are expensive – the Queen gets around £5 million a year towards the expenses of the 400 people who make up the royal household.

- Their political duties are meaningless – even the Queen's speech for the annual opening of Parliament is written by the Prime Minister.

- There is an argument that Heads of State should all be elected, if we are a true democracy, as happens in other countries with a similar system to Britain.

- The royals represent a time in history when Britain took over far flung countries 'discovered' by explorers, made the British monarchy their ruler, and exploited them for their precious resources such as spices or gold. Colonialization, as it is called, has no place in Britain's international relationships today.

- The royals stand for wealth and privilege, which is the very opposite of equality and modern society. Many people in Britain do not respect or want a Royal Family any more.

The Queen's Coronation, 1953. The Queen and the Royal Family have been widely criticized for being out of touch with modern society and values, yet they still enjoy huge international popularity.

THE ROYAL FAMILY?

NO: ● The Royal Family brings a lot of money into Britain, from tourists who want to see the ceremonies such as the changing of the Guard at Buckingham Palace.

● The Queen, in particular, is a brilliant non-political representative of British good will. She makes hundreds of visits abroad every year, and people flock to see her. Her trips abroad also mean that the Prime Minister and other key members of Parliament have fewer diplomatic engagements and can be in the UK more often to do their jobs.

● The Queen is head of the group of countries known as the Commonwealth, and brings them together to gain strength from being part of a group.

● The Royal Family represents strong British traditions, which make us different from other nations — they are an important part of our identity.

● The Queen has weekly meetings with the Prime Minister — perhaps her many years of advising Prime Ministers enable her to pass on useful advice.

Why should we care about democracy?

What is a democracy?

In most countries, including Britain, Australia and the United States of America, the citizens choose their government by voting in elections. The government system is based on treating all its citizens equally. This system is known as **democracy**. India is the world's largest democracy, and it can take up to three weeks to complete the process of counting the votes in their general election because so much of the country has poor transport and communication links.

Why is democracy important?

Most people feel that a government is more likely to make **laws** and represent what the majority of its people want if it knows that those same people can replace it every five years, as in Britain. Governments that do not need the vote of the people can concentrate on making themselves more powerful, knowing that their people have no power to change the situation. They may spend lots of money on the latest weapons which technology can provide or on expensive buildings to enhance their own power, while people starve to death.

What are the alternatives?

A government which does not run on choice is known as an autocracy. In some countries, one person, a small group or the army might take control of government. This may happen by force. In this situation, or when a leader suddenly decides to start making all the decisions on their own, having previously worked with a democratic system, the government becomes a dictatorship. Saddam Hussein in Iraq is a dictator, just as Hitler was in Germany, from the mid-1930s until the end of the Second World War in 1945.

Some countries claim to be democracies, but the voters have no faith in the honesty of their election system. In 1999 Indonesia held their first democratic elections in more than 30 years, and people held demonstrations in the streets because they were suspicious about the vote counting. In the presidential elections in Nigeria in 1994, the army declared that the election was discounted because they did not favour the **candidate** they thought would win.

In some countries, such as in Jordan in the Middle East, or Morocco in North Africa, the **monarchy** governs. In the UK, the governing power of the monarchy was limited in the thirteenth century with the signing of the Magna Carta.

Democracy is more than voting

Beyond a democratic system for choosing government, the UK has many ways of encouraging people to challenge the Government, both locally and nationally, if they want to see something changed in society (see page 42). This is a crucial aspect of democracy.

Should we be made to vote?

In Australia, everybody has to vote by law. Voters are allowed to make a blank vote if they do not want to vote for any of the candidates. Do you think people in Britain should be made to vote? Does it go against true democracy to make people vote by law?

FACT

● *50% of 18–24 year-olds did not vote in the last general election and 60% did not vote in local elections.*

State of the Young Nation *survey by the British Youth Council, 1998*

Citizens queue for hours in the heat to vote in South Africa's first fully democratic elections in 1994, when black people were given the right to vote.

CITIZEN POWER

In South Africa, democracy was seen as the way to end the domination of black citizens by white citizens. Only white citizens were allowed to vote until 1994, when black people gained the right to vote. Nelson Mandela was voted in to head up South Africa's first democratic government and to start the process of giving black people equal rights in all aspects of society.

Free speech and censorship

Should citizens be allowed to express their ideas, even if they are **abusing** other people? There is a political party in Britain called the National Front, for example, which is strongly **racist** against anybody who is not white. Some people think it should not be allowed to exist.

Free speech

The eighteenth-century French writer and thinker Voltaire said: 'I do not agree with what you say but I would die for your right to say it.' In many countries people are not allowed to speak out if they disagree with the views of their government. The **pressure group** Amnesty International campaigns for the

Peaceful demonstrations are one way that people can express views which might be different from their government or from the majority of other citizens. Such demonstrations, like this one against hunting, are an important aspect of democracy, but are not allowed in some countries.

release of thousands of people all over the world whose governments have imprisoned them because of their political opinions.

In Britain, freedom of speech is valued as one of the main rights of citizens. Most people were horrified in 1989 when the leader of the Islamic Church in Iran, the

Ayatollah Kohmeini, announced that the Indian writer Salman Rushdie, who lives in Britain, should be put to death because parts of his book *The Satanic Verses* offended the Muslim religion. Copies of the book were publicly burned by Muslims, and Rushdie had to go into hiding for nearly ten years before the threat was lifted by the next Muslim leader.

The most famous symbol of free speech in Britain is Speaker's Corner in London's Hyde Park. Anybody can stand on what is known as a 'soap box' and address the listening crowd on a Sunday morning. Many important people in the history of politics, including Marx and Lenin, have visited Speaker's Corner.

Censorship

Governments put varying levels of control on what information reaches their citizens. This is called censorship. In Britain, there is censorship on entertainment. Television programmes containing sex, violence and swearing cannot be shown before 9.00 pm, because they are considered unsuitable for a young audience, and some films are restricted to viewers over the age of 18. There is a lot of debate about whether pornography (showing very intimate sexual activity) should be banned. Some people believe it damages the way women are treated in society because most of it **exploits** women.

In some countries newspapers may be banned and both China and Singapore, for example, have blocked out Internet sites about **politics** and human rights. Do you think we should have more or less censorship in this country?

Speaker's Corner in London stands for the right of free speech. Crowds gather on Sunday mornings to see who will get onto a 'soap box' to express their views on an issue.

FREEDOM OF INFORMATION ACT

The British Parliament is working on a Freedom of Information Act which will allow citizens to get more information held by the government. In addition to this, the new Data Protection Act, introduced in Spring 2000, gives people the right to see records about themselves held on computer files. Views differ about what sorts of records the public should be allowed to see. Protecting people's **privacy** also needs to be considered.

What can you do to improve where you live?

People living in countries like Britain, America and Australia, have an easy life in many ways. If we want to go somewhere, we just use one of many different kinds of transport; we only have to press a button on the CD player to hear our favourite music; we can eat immediately we feel hungry at a choice of fast-food restaurants. Sadly, our countries are doing the most damage to the planet. That means that we all need to do our bit to improve the environment and reduce **pollution**.

In our neighbourhood, it is also important to have surroundings that are pleasant to look at and make everybody who lives there feel proud to be part of the **community**. A bed of flowers cheering up a concrete landscape may do more to spread positive feelings about where we live than we might think, and in turn spur people on to make even more effort with their surroundings.

Isn't it the government's job to improve where we live?

There are certainly some things that can only be done by the government or your **local council**, such as controlling car traffic, increasing the number of recycling points, or making housing estates look more welcoming. But that does not mean that everybody else should sit back and complain.

CASE STUDY: COMMUNITY ACTION

Thirteen year-old Mark Bibby has been helping an organization called Butterfly Conservation by recording the number and types of butterfly he sees in his local area. His records will be combined with others to work out the overall spread of butterflies in Britain and how to preserve them for future generations.

Counting butterflies is one of hundreds of different environmental projects that young people are taking part in around the country to give the planet a better future.

CATALYSTS FOR ACTION

Here are some suggestions, but why not make the most of something you are already interested in, such as Mark's butterfly project.

- Get permission and gather a group of friends to paint a wall of your local community centre or school in a scene using bright, sunny colours. Your mural will cheer up everybody who walks past it.

- If there is scrubland that could be turned into a public garden, join or start a project to transform it with plants and flowers – your local community group or council should be able to help you organize it.

- Walk to school, or cycle, to help reduce pollution and local traffic. Perhaps start a campaign to get a bike shed at school if there isn't one.

Painting a mural brightens a dull corner of a housing estate and increases the participants' feeling of belonging to their local community.

Doing your bit can be easy and fun

Young people are taking part in activities to improve where they live in all kinds of ways, and by joining them you could learn new skills, make new friends and have a lot of fun as well as doing your bit for your neighbourhood.

While you are making big plans, do not forget to do your bit closer to home. Pick up litter, recycle newspapers, glass, plastic, aluminium and textiles, do not waste water and electricity, and avoid buying things which have lots of packaging – every little effort like this helps the environment.

What can you do to help others?

Looking out for other people makes you a good neighbour, a good friend, a good member of your family, and a good citizen. Keep your eyes open as you walk around and you will see people who could do with a helping hand. Maybe there is a young mother trying to carry a pushchair up some steps, or an older person struggling with their shopping bag. Your help could make their day!

Apart from acting spontaneously, there are lots of ways to join an organized project to help other people (see below). Being a **volunteer** can be very rewarding and great fun, but make sure you plan it carefully so that you are happy to take on responsibility and ready to give up your free time.

What some other young people are doing…

Helping run an anti-bullying campaign at school

Acland Burghley School has an Anti-Bullying Campaign (ABC), with students trained to be counsellors. Any pupil worried about bullying can see a counsellor in private. Counsellors are given guidance by adults, who oversee the project. Counsellors try to help someone who is being bullied to think about their good points as an individual and to feel more self-confident in the face of being bullied. They sometimes find people come to them admitting that they are bullies themselves. Counsellors feel that there is an unwritten 'zero tolerance of bullying' atmosphere in the school, thanks to the ABC, and more respect between **peers**. The ABC has won a Good Citizen award from the **local council**.

Giving telephone advice to other young people

Youth2Youth is a national telephone helpline run by young people (see page 46 for details). Anyone over the age of 14 can apply to be a **volunteer**. Volunteers are trained in how to listen to other young people talking through their problems and they give up two hours a fortnight of their free time to answer the phone.

SOME QUESTIONS TO ASK YOURSELF BEFORE BECOMING A VOLUNTEER

- How much time do I want to give?
- Do I want to volunteer with my mates or on my own?
- Do I want to try a new situation, or is there something I am already doing that I could build on? (Perhaps you already visit one older person in hospital, for example.)
- What skills have I got to offer? (You may be a good listener, for example.)
- Will it be easy and safe for me to get there and back on my own?

Creating projects which help others

Around 100 schools and youth groups across Britain have joined an organization called Changemakers, which helps young people to make up their own activities as volunteers. One group of 14-year-old boys ran an anti-**racism** campaign in Newcastle and signed up the city's football team stars to back them up.

Giving telephone counselling to another young person in need involves a big commitment to giving up spare time and learning new skills, but most volunteers find the rewards are well worth their efforts.

CHECK OUT YOUR OPTIONS

- Find out what is happening locally – your nearest youth project or volunteer bureau should be able to point you in the right direction.

- Talk to other people about whether they know of any opportunities.

- Before you commit yourself to an organization, find out what their expectations are of their volunteers, how flexible they are about when and how you volunteer, and whether there are opportunities for progression with time.

- Ask if you can go along and sit in on an evening to see what the work is like before you commit yourself.

Have your say

You are far more likely to want to be a good citizen, and to do your bit to help make society a better place if you feel that your views and concerns are taken seriously. There are lots of opportunities to get your opinions across to the people who make the important decisions – it just takes a bit of thought and effort.

Have your say in school

In school, you can write for your school newspaper and get involved in your school council, as well as talking to teachers about your ideas for improving the school **community**. You could even ask to do a presentation to the governors about your ideas, with a group of **peers** who share the same views.

PRESSURE GROUPS

Pressure groups are organizations that use the support of the public and the **media** to put pressure on the government to change **policies** and **laws**. They may organize letter-writing campaigns and protest marches, and also work quietly with the government when that is needed. Examples of pressure groups with strong support from young people include Amnesty International, who campaign for human rights, Friends of the Earth and Greenpeace, who campaign for protection of the environment, the Royal Society for Prevention of Cruelty to Animals (RSPCA), and the British Red Cross and Oxfam, who work to relieve poverty internationally and provide emergency services for **refugees** due to war or other disasters.

Have your say in the wider world

It is easy to feel powerless as a teenager, but the government and other organizations are increasingly proving that they take young people seriously as citizens. Camden Council in London is just one example. The council recently gathered a group of 18 young people, aged 14–21, to find out what their main concerns were and to give them a say in the council's plans. It was discovered, for example, that there was a gap in plans on filling leisure time. Council department plans now say how they will meet young people's aims.

FACTS

- *One in ten 12–25 year-olds have been on a protest march.*

  2020 Vision *survey by the Industrial Society, 1997*

- *MPs get 200–300 letters a week from citizens who want them to use their influence to change something.*

There is a saying that knowledge is power, and finding out as much as you can about the issue that infuriates or excites you will strengthen your ability to have influence in whatever way you choose.

So, if you feel strongly about something…

Remember that if everybody does one thing to further a cause that is important to them, that would mean over 50 million activities in Britain alone – a great deal of citizen power.

Glossary

abducted taken away by someone using force, as in kidnapping

abolish put an end to

abuse treating someone else badly or taking unfair advantage of them

ballot a secret vote marked on an official printed slip of paper, and placed in an official box, which is later opened for counting the votes

candidates individuals for whom people may vote in an election

care short for 'a care home', which is an alternative home to living with a family and run by the council. A **carer** is the person who plays the role of parent.

civil liberties the right to express oneself in thought, word and action as a free citizen

civil servants people who work for the government, who are appointed in the same way as an employee of a business rather than being elected

community neighbourhood or place where people share in common activities, such as a school

cult a religious system outside of the widely established religions, often involving excessive admiration of one person

currency type of money used in a country, such as pounds sterling in England, or dollars in Australia

democracy a form of government where people collectively hold the power (because it is they who vote for the government), and which recognizes equal rights

democratic recognizing equal rights of citizens

discrimination treating people differently, usually badly, because they are different from yourself or the group you belong to. Groups often discriminated against include disabled people and people from racial minority backgrounds.

drug abuse misusing drugs in a way that may cause you harm

election manifesto a statement of what a political party promises to do if it is elected as the next government

employers people or companies who pay others to work for them

ethnic minorities people from races which are not the dominant one

European Union a group formed between governments with the main aim of improving their overall economy. Fifteen European countries are members.

evidence facts and objects used to prove something

exploitation taking advantage of somebody or something for your own benefit

guidelines a list of suggestions or instructions

immigration moving into a country with the intention of settling there permanently

law a rule which is created by the government

lobbying seeking to influence parliamentarians. The term derives from the 'lobby' – the area MPs walk through on their way to the official chambers of the Houses of Parliament.

local council government for your village, town or city

media the organizations which communicate news, such as television, radio, newspapers and magazines

ministers MPs in government who are responsible for a particular area, such as health

monarchy royalty

Moonies members of the Unification Church, led by Sun Myung Moon

neglect when parents or carers do not provide children with proper clothing, food, warmth, shelter, care and protection

opposition parties those political parties that have not been elected to run the government

opinion polls surveys which ask a number of people what they think about issues so they can find out the majority viewpoint

peers people of similar age, for example people in the same class at school

policies written plans and aims

politics a broad term which covers all aspects of government

polling station a public place where people vote in elections

pollution damage caused to all aspects of the environment, such as the air, oceans or forests, by harmful gases from car exhausts, factories and other sources

prejudice judging somebody, usually on the basis of their physical appearance or beliefs, without knowing them

pressure groups organizations which work to persuade the government to make changes

privacy being allowed to be by yourself, or have your own thoughts and opinions

racist somebody who treats others differently because of their race

redundant losing a job because there is no longer sufficient work

refugees people forced to flee to another country because of war or famine, or because of not having civil liberties

sexual exploitation using somebody for sex

sexuality whether someone is sexually attracted to someone of the opposite sex, their own sex, or either sex

State an organized community under one government

sub-culture a small group within society, which the majority of people have nothing to do with

tabloids smaller-sized newspapers, which concentrate on less serious news and are sometimes called 'the red tops' because of the splash of red across most of their fronts

terrorists people who use violence to fight for a cause

United Nations (UN) an international association of states which was set up in 1945, following the Second World War, to maintain peace and develop friendly relations between member nations, and promote human rights

volunteer someone who does unpaid work in order to help others

Contacts and helplines

AMNESTY INTERNATIONAL

99-119 Rosebery Avenue, London, EC1R 4RE
020 7814 6200 – Campaigns on human rights issues.

THE BRITISH YOUTH COUNCIL

020 7278 0582 – Has information on how young people can get involved in decision-making.

BUTTERFLY CONSERVATION

PO Box 222, Dedham, Essex, C07 6EY. Send a stamped addressed envelope (31p) for a free information pack.

CHANGEMAKERS

9 Mansfield Place, London, NW3 1HS
020 7431 1412 – Works with schools and youth groups to encourage young people to create their own volunteer projects.

CHILDLINE

Freepost 1111, London, N1 0BR
0800 1111 – 24 hour helpline. Children can phone or write with a problem of any kind.

CHILDREN'S EXPRESS

Exmouth House, 3-11 Pine Street, London, EC1R 0JH
020 7833 2577 – News Agency for young volunteer journalists.

THE CITIZENSHIP FOUNDATION

15 St Swithins Lane, London, EC4N 8AL
020 7929 3344 – www.citfou.org.uk
Promotes citizenship through a wide range of programmes.

CRE (THE COMMISSION FOR RACIAL EQUALITY)

Elliott House, 10-12 Allington Street, London, SW1E 5EH.
London *020 7828 7022*; Edinburgh *0131 226 5186*;
Cardiff *029 2038 8977* – Works to stop racist behaviour and support protection laws.

THE COURT SERVICE

Southside, 105 Victoria Street, London, SW1E 6QT
020 7210 1775/2009/2200 – Information about the court system, or what to do if you are a victim of crime.

GREENPEACE

Canonbury Villas, London, N1 2PN
020 7865 8100 – Campaigns for protection of the environment.

ENVIRONMENT AGENCY

Rio House, Waterside Drive, Aztec West, Almondsbury, Bristol, BS32 4UD
01454 624400 – Runs free 24 hour phone line for reporting any environmental incident: *0800 80 70 60*.

EUROPEAN PARLIAMENT INFORMATION OFFICE

2 Queen Anne's Gate, London, SW1H 9AA
020 7227 4300 – Information about MEPs etc.

FRIENDS OF THE EARTH

26-28 Underwood Street, London, N1 7JQ
020 7490 1555 – Campaigns for protection of the environment.

THE HOUSE OF COMMONS INFORMATION OFFICE

6th Floor, Norman Shaw Building North, London, SW1A 2TT *020 7219 2105*, www.parliament.uk/commons – Provides information about MPs, how the Commons works etc.

KIDSCAPE

152 Buckingham Palace Road, London, SW1 9TR
020 7730 3300 – Gives advice on keeping safe, preventing bullying etc. Send large stamped addressed envelope for information pack.

THE NATIONAL CHILDREN'S BUREAU

8 Wakely Street, London, EC1V 7QE
020 7843 6000 – www.ncb.org.uk
Works to identify and promote the well-being and interests of all children across every aspect of their lives.

NSPCC (National Society for the Prevention of Cruelty to Children)

National Centre, 42 Curtain Road, London, EC2A 3NH
020 7825 2500 – Runs the Child Protection Helpline: *0800 800 500*.

OXFAM

274 Banbury Road, Oxford, OX2 7DZ
01865 311311. Works to relieve poverty internationally, and campaigns on the causes of poverty.

RSPCA (Royal Society for the Prevention of Cruelty to Animals)

Causeway, Horsham, West Sussex, RH12 1HG
01403 264 181 – Has a 24 hour emergency line to report an animal in distress tel: *0990 555 999*

SAVE THE CHILDREN

17 Grove Lane, London, SE5 8RD
020 7703 5400 – Works for a fairer world for children, has information on working children.

YOUTH2YOUTH

020 8896 3675 – e-mail help@youth2youth.co.uk.
www.youth2youth.co.uk – Helpline for young people, run by young people.

IN AUSTRALIA

AUSTRALIAN ELECTORAL COMMISSION

www.aec.gov.au – Has information about the electoral system in Australia and how to register to vote.

PARLIAMENTARY EDUCATION OFFICE

www.peo.gov.au – Has information about the Australian parliamentary system and key personnel as well as civics in general.

ENVIRONMENTAL PROTECTION AUTHORITY

www.epa.vic.gov.au (Victoria)
www.epa.nsw.gov.au (New South Wales)
Runs the EPA Pollution Watch Line – For reporting any instances of abuse of your environment: *03 9695 2777*.

CRIME STOPPERS

Runs freecall line on which you can make a confidential report about criminal offenses you have witnessed: *1800 333 000*.

CHILD PROTECTION SERVICE

13 1278

KIDS HELPLINE

1800 551800 – call free for advice and support.

REACH OUT

www.reachout.asn.au - helps children with a variety of problems.

SAVE THE CHILDREN, AUSTRALIA

PO Box 1281, Collingwood, VIC 3066

Additional web sites

www.vois.org.uk – A web site with links to individual charities and advice on volunteering.
www. scottish.parliament.uk – Information about the Scottish Parliament aimed at young people.
www.bbc.co.uk – Access to up to the minute news and current affairs.

Note: the Internet has hundreds of sites you can visit to find out more about organizations and issues which you have read about in this book. If you enter a search word or phrase, such as 'human rights', several sites will be highlighted for you.

Further reading

Reading

A Fight to Belong
Alan Gibbons
Save the Children

A Guide to Rights
Save the Children, 1994

Contemporary Moral Issues
Joe Jenkins
Heinemann, 1998

Rights in the Home
E Haughton and P Clarke
Franklin Watts, 1997

Rights of Women
Mandy Wharton
Franklin Watts, 1988

What are Children's Rights?
Craig Donnellan
Independence, Issues for the Nineties series, 1996

Young Opinions, Great Ideas
views of 70 young people aged 10–17 years throughout England on their concerns and views on how they can influence change
From the National Children's Bureau, 1998

Other Sources

What is Parliament?
Video from the Parliamentary Channel, 160 Great Portland Street, London W1N 5TB

Parliament Past and Present
Permanent exhibition about the work and history of the House of Commons and House of Lords, Jewel Tower, Westminster (020 7222 2219).

Index